Fucking Love Yourself

An adult coloring book of self-care ideas and mandala designs.

ISBN 978-0-9863098-4-7

Author + Illustrator: Alexandra Love Sarton

www.alexandra.love

Fucking Love
Yourself

Get the Fuck
Out of Your
Own Way

Lighten
the Fuck
Up Sometimes

Stop Fucking
Doubting Yourself

Say What You
Fucking Feel

Have Some
Fucking Patience
With Yourself

Be
Fucking
Honest

Be Fucking
Nice To Yourself

Create Genuine
Fucking Moments

Laugh Until
You Can't
Fucking Breathe

Be Fucking
Passionate

Compliment
The Fuck
Outta Yourself

Believe in Your
Fucking Greatness

Always Do Your
Fucking Best

Don't Take Things
Fucking Personally

Trust Your
Fucking Intuition

Use Your
Fucking
Imagination

Appreciate
Your Entire
Fucking Body

Smile Much
Fucking More

Give Authentic
Fucking Hugs

Be Direct
About Your
Fucking Boundaries

Develop A
Regular Fucking
Spiritual Practice

Cultivate Your
Inner Fucking
Awareness

Listen To Beautiful
Fucking Music

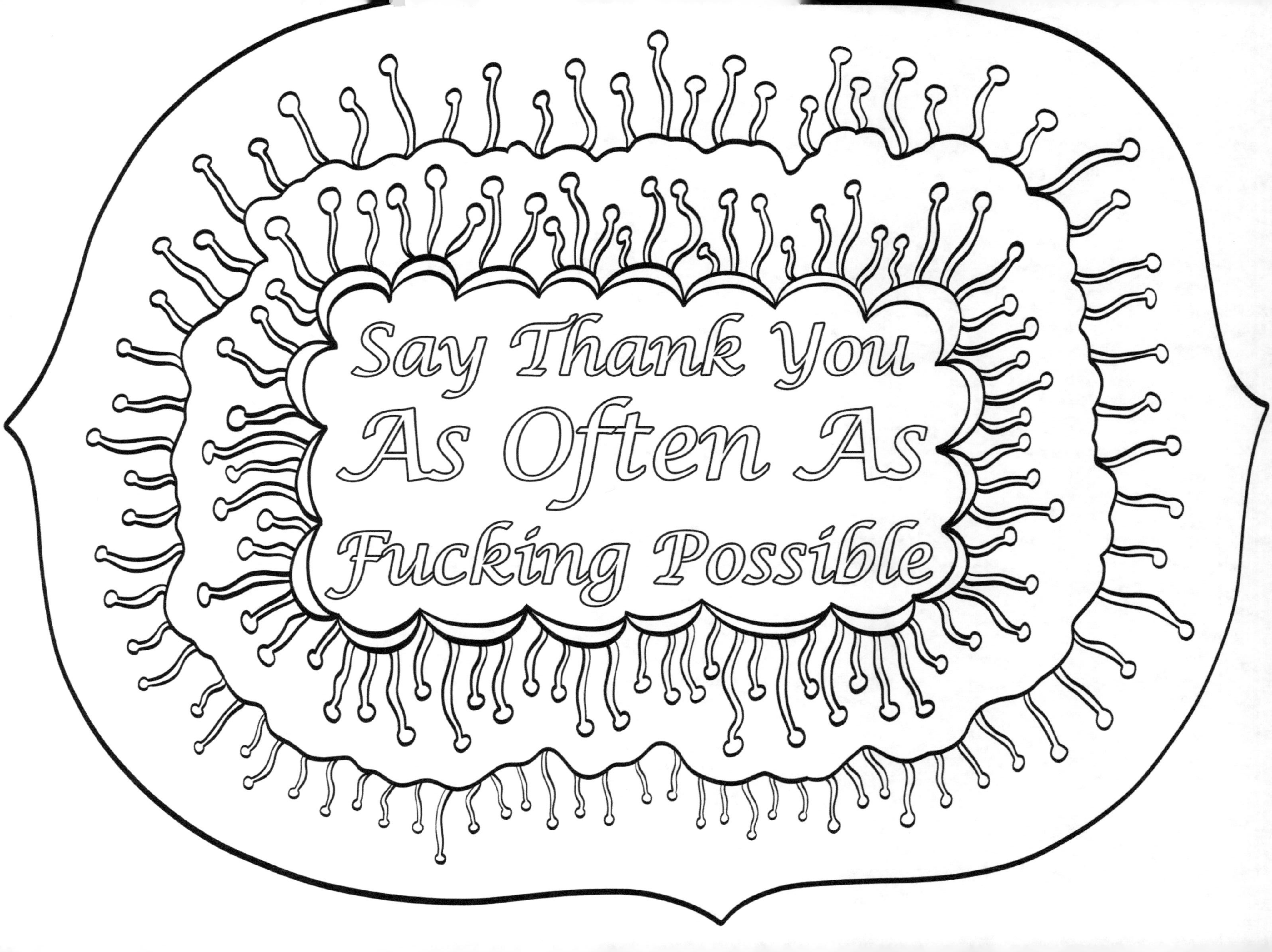
Say Thank You
As Often As
Fucking Possible

Make Fucking
Eye Contact
With People

Envision Your
Future Being
Beautiful As Fuck

Leave Yourself
Little Fucking
Love Notes

Experience
Fucking Solitude

Rest When You
Want To
Fucking Rest

Allow Yourself
To Be Fully
Fucking Loved

www.ingramcontent.com/pod-product-compliance
Lightning Source LLC
Chambersburg PA
CBHW060519300426
44112CB00017B/2733
* 9 7 8 0 9 8 6 3 0 9 8 4 7 *